PROTEAS IN HAWAII

Distributed in Australia by
RED HILL PROTEA
RMB 3333 McIlroys Rd., Red Hill
Vic 3937 Australia
Fax (059) 892382 / Tel (059) 892389

Sugarbush *(Protea repens)* glows from within as though lit by a deeply embedded light.

Text and Design by Angela Kay Kepler
Photography by Jacob R. Mau

Mutual Publishing

As they mature, these handsome "rockets" *(Leucospermum reflexum)* unfurl their "pins" outward and downward, revealing a succession of resplendent colors.

Text © 1988 by Angela Kay Kepler
Photographs © 1988 by Jacob Mau
COPYRIGHT © 1988 by Mutual Publishing
1127 11th Avenue, Mezz. B
Honolulu, Hawaii 96816
Ph (808) 732-1709 • Fax (808) 734-4094
Email: mutual@lava.net • Url: http://www.pete.com/mutual

Cover design by Jane Hopkins
Printed in Japan

TABLE OF CONTENTS

cont'd

A close-up of "fresh protea in the round" (back cover), showing a variety
of proteas, pincushions, banksias and leucadendrons (foliage proteas).

TABLE OF CONTENTS (continued)

A small, delicate protea, blushing bride *(Serruria florida)* is occasionally used in South African wedding bouquets.

The brilliant reds, oranges, and yellows of the Veldfire pincushion (a *Leucospermum* hybrid) dazzle the eye, recalling an African veld (savannah) bush fire.

ACKNOWLEDGEMENTS

This book was produced in collaboration with the following organizations: Davis Farm Enterprises, Ehu Farm, Hapapa Farm, Hawaii Protea Cooperative, Hunalani Farm, Mauka-McKay Protea Farm, Olinda Vista Nursery, Protea Gardens of Maui, Proteas of Hawaii, Maui Sunburst, Protea Gift Shoppe, Sunrise Protea Farm, Upcountry Protea Farm and Wolford Kula Farm.

We are especially grateful to Susan and Lonnie Hardesty (Proteas of Hawaii), Cindy Lawrence (Hawaii Protea Cooperative), Joan Mercer (Ehu Farm), Paul Winiarski, and Dr. Philip Parvin (University of Hawaii Agricultural Research Center) for ·their enthusiastic support, assistance in flower selection and loan, and manuscript comments. Eileen and Kathy of Exotica Design Maui kindly created the flower arrangement. Thanks are also due to my husband Cameron, who not only provided useful comments on the manuscript but, due to work obligations, lived apart from his family for months during its preparation. Lastly, I would like to express personal *aloha* to Jacob Mau for his positive energy and perfectionism which contributed to the splendid photographs in this book.

No wonder this "firefly" hybrid and other similar pincushions are called "sunbursts" in Hawaii! This name has supplanted the original South African name—nodding pincushion.

INTRODUCTION

Proteas, the curious botanical novelties which today are such an integral part of Hawaii's exotic flower industry, come in a dazzling array of shapes, sizes and textures: furry pink powderpuffs, bursts of orange fireworks, fleecy "pinecones," silky balls of cerise tissue sporting feathery eyelashes, looped corncobs, golden spiky acorns, and even "stuffed animals" with curly fur. Their flowerheads range in size from a few millimeters across to dignified whoppers that top 12" in diameter.

This book covers a representative sampling of 44 species and hybrids (plus many color forms) most likely encountered in Hawaiian gift-boxes, at florists, flower farms or in floral displays. With the enormous recent popularity of Hawaii-grown proteas, however, these flowers have been mistakenly associated with the tropics. Proteas are neither tropical nor native to Hawaii.

The protea family (pronounced *PRO*-tee-uh not pro-*TAY*-uh), which includes true proteas, banksias, foilage proteas (leucadendrons), pincushions, and dryandras, is native to the Southern Hemisphere, primarily South Africa and Australia. Two groups are most notable: the fancy true proteas (genus *Protea*, over 100 species), which hail originally from the southernmost tip of Africa, and the banksias (genus *Banksia*, 73 species) from Australia.

Almost all cultivated proteas closely resemble those in wild situations. This is in sharp contrast to many garden and nursery flowers (for example, roses, chrysanthemums), which have undergone many years of hybridization and improvement over their (often puny) originals. A drive around the Cape Province of South Africa is enhanced by thousands of protea bushes carpeting savannahs, craggy canyons, steep ridges, and high mountain peaks. Australia is similar. When I was growing up in Sydney in the 1950s I remember collecting wildflowers such as banksias and waratahs (both members of the protea family) from the nearby "bush."

Today in Hawaii, proteas (a general term for all family members of the Proteaceae) grow on the cool volcanic slopes of 10,000' Haleakala, Maui and 13,000' Mauna Kea, Big Island (see map below). These pleasant, upcountry, Mediterranean-type climates at 2,000' to 4,000' elevation are dry with frequent cloud cover, cool evening temperatures, and plenty of daytime sun. Slightly acidic soils, local mountain breezes, and excellent natural drainage complete the requirements for optimum growing conditions. As horticultural techniques in Hawaii become more refined, island-grown proteas each year set new world standards for superiority, rivaling the beauty and perfection of flowers from their original habitats.

Hill banksia *(Banksia collina)*, a rare variety with black loops.

Hawaii's Protea-Growing Areas

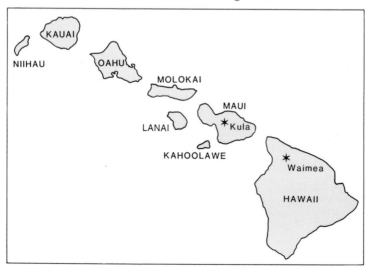

Now called "pink mink," *Protea neriifolia* was the first protea ever described. Many color forms, all with soft, sensual fur, are grown commercially in Hawaii today.

AN HISTORICAL UNFOLDING

Mountaineering, adventure, royal greenhouses—perhaps these are not concepts normally associated with proteas. Island residents and visitors today relate them more with spacious hotel lobbies adorned with elegant flower arrangements, oblong gift-boxes, memorable trips to upcountry farms or perhaps a lei of golden pincushions around a dignitary's neck.

Who would have dreamed that Maui's "pink mink," gathered by an adventurous sailor along Africa's Cape coast, was one of the first plants ever described outside Europe, or that 16th Century explorers rounding the Cape of Good Hope picked basketfuls of sugarbush flowers with which to sweeten their foods. Similarly, who could have guessed that notable historic figures such as England's King George III and France's Empress Josephine (Napoleon's wife) enjoyed cultivating proteas as their primary hobbies. By the time Captain Cook arrived in Hawaii in 1778, King George was already admiring king proteas in London's Kew Gardens.

Captain Cook himself played an important role in the early discovery of proteaceous plants. On his 1770 voyage to Australia, Cook's surgeon-naturalist, Sir Joseph Banks, discovered several strange species of plants which were later named *Banksias.* When Captain Cook sighted the Hawaiian Islands, he may well have wondered if banksias grew there too.

Although King George's passion for these unknown wildflowers propelled them into European celebrities, technological advances in Europe sealed their fate, at least temporarily. At first the old-fashioned, furnace-heated greenhouses of the nobility provided optimum indoor conditions—plenty of heat and dryness. However, when steam heat metamorphosed them into tropical jungles, the proteas expired. Thus their first scintillating era of horticultural splendor became quickly relegated to history as plant fanciers diverted their attentions to other exotics such as orchids and bromeliads, which thrived in the jungly atmosphere of the "improved" greenhouses.

After a century of virtual neglect, protea interest rekindled in South Africa in 1913. In 1930, a commercial nursery appeared, and by the 1960s South Africa was once again exporting proteas to Europe, this time as nursery seedlings and cut flowers rather than precious seeds earmarked for royalty.

During the 1960s pincushions were planted in California and New Zealand. Maui followed quickly. David Williams, pioneering these floral oddities in Hawaii, planted 50 species on the Kula slopes of Haleakala. His successor as superintendent of the University of Hawaii's Agricultural Experiment Station, Dr. Philip Parvin, became so enthused with the idea he is now considered the foremost authority on protea farming in the United States. As chairman of the Protea Working Group, International Society for Horticultural Science, and founding secretary of the International Protea Association, Parvin has been responsible for focusing world attention on Hawaii's new flower industry. Financial support from the State of Hawaii has assisted its growth into a multi-million-dollar enterprise, with 90 percent of protea blooms originating on Maui.

"Sunburst" (*Leucospermum cordifolium*).

NOMENCLATURE

Many members of the protea family have undergone recent name changes in Hawaii, in association with the booming floriculture trade. Some names are recognized internationally; others are not. Many are already entrenched in trade vocabulary, as it has been proven that part of Hawaii's success in selling proteas is due not only to the spectacular flowers themselves but to their appealing names. In addition, some species, varieties, and hybrids had never previously been assigned common names.

In deference to protea growers worldwide, private and commercial outlets that are confused about names, and dismayed scientists, horticulturalists, and nurserymen, I have attempted, with the help of Dr. Parvin, to standardize the names used in Hawaii.

Within botany and horticulture, certain rules of nomenclature need to be followed to allow for accuracy and communication. This applies to both common and scientific names. Nomenclature in this book follows standard international rules, with a variation allowing for the recognition of names originating in Hawaii. (Normally the first names assigned to a plant are expected to be kept and used in all literature.) NEW MARKETABLE NAMES ORIGINATING IN HAWAII ARE PRINTED IN QUOTATION MARKS IN THIS BOOK, for example South Africa's oleander-leaved protea *(Protea neriifolia)* is called by its Hawaiian marketing name "pink mink."

This next section clarifies name-usage. I urge that it be read by anyone interested in protea names, especially those in the trade:
1. The PRINCIPAL COMMON NAME (bold capitals) is the accepted one. Please use in preference to any other English name, especially if you live in Hawaii or the U.S. mainland. Plant names are not capitalized unless a proper noun is present, e.g. Menzies' or firewood banksia. *If in quotes, it is a new commercial name originating in Hawaii,* most of which are now accepted by the International Protea Association, e.g. "ermine tail" for long-leaved protea.
2. The SCIENTIFIC NAME (in italics) is the currently accepted one. This is the *only* standard name. *The first part (genus or generic name) is capitalized and the second part (specific name) is not capitalized.* Traditionally both parts are underlined or italicized, e.g. *Protea magnifica.* If part of the scientific name is in parentheses, this indicates an old name commonly found in the literature, e.g. *P. magnifica (=barbigera).* Note here that it is not necessary to write out

the genus each time, e.g. within an account or paragraph about *Protea magnifica,* it is written in full the first time and thereafter contracted to *P. magnifica.* In the protea trade, growers communicate using the second part of the scientific name, rather than the common name, e.g. *compacta* for *Protea compacta,* the "prince." *Flowers are listed under these names in catalogs.*
3. The section OTHER NAMES includes names by which the plant is known in its native country, e.g. queen protea is also called giant woolly-beard or woolly-headed protea in South Africa. Names in quotes (not principal common names) are alternate marketing names. Some of these minor names have been used by only one farm in Hawaii.
4. Words after the scientific name, preceded by cv, denote a NAMED HORTICULTURAL VARIETY OR HYBRID, and are usually capitalized but not underlined or italicized. Whether there are quotes around the cultivar/ hybrid name depends on whether the name originated in Hawaii or not, e.g. *Protea obtusifolia* cv Greenvalley Red is from South Africa and *Protea eximia* cv "Rose-spoon" is from Hawaii. In some literature, single quotes are placed around cultivar names.
5. FOR NATURAL SPECIES, ENGLISH NAMES SHOULD NOT BE MIXED WITH SCIENTIFIC NAMES, e.g. *Protea* "White Mink" is not acceptable. In this case the plant's natural white form, named in Hawaii, is written thus: *Protea neriifolia* cv "White Mink" or merely "white mink" (note that the cultivar is capitalized when attached to the scientific name, but not capitalized when used as a common name). When hybrids have been formed from two good species, forming a reproductively viable plant (naturally or horticulturally), the following is permissible: *Leucospermum* cv Hawaii Gold, a contraction of *Leucospermum conocarpodendron X L. cuneiforme* cv Hawaii Gold. Here there are no quotes around Hawaii Gold, as this is the hybrid's original and sole name, and *Leucospermum* is contracted to *L.* for the second species.
6. A TRUE SPECIES SHOULD NEVER BE CALLED A VARIETY. Varieties are forms of a true species which differ from the usual plant in shape, color, leaf-form, etc. For example, queen protea is normally pink, but also has naturally occurring varieties in cerise, chartreuse, orange, and white. Within these color variations, further varieties occur with white, and gold-and-white fur trimmings.

TRUE PROTEAS

Yellow mink *(Protea neriifolia)*.

A WORD ABOUT PROTEAS

Proteas rank among the most ancient plants in the world. Dating from fossils over 300 million years old, they number approximately 1,500 species and varieties.

The name "protea" is derived from the scientific name *Protea*, which in turn has legendary roots in the Greek god Proteus, a remarkable creature who was able to change himself into innumerable shapes. Such an appropriate name alludes to the extraordinary diversity and specialization of the protea family.

In the following pages I have attempted to use everyday language. However, as proteas are very different from ordinary flowers, their structure may be difficult to understand. An unfamiliar word which needs clarification is *bract: Each protea bloom is not a single flower but a tight mound of filamentous, modified flowers surrounded by brightly colored, petal-like leaves called bracts. As proteas have no petals, what you think are petals are the bracts.*

The entire make-up of a protea is very similar to that of the unrelated artichoke. The fleshy, edible portions of an artichoke, occurring in several layers around the "heart," are also bracts, and the tight, spiky filaments that you scrape off the "heart" are its mass of flowers, so modified that only their basic reproductive structures remain.

This first section of the book covers the true proteas (*Protea* species), showpieces of the family. Pincushions, foliage proteas (leucadendrons), and banksias are constructed somewhat differently

and are explained in their appropriate sections.

For additional reading, I recommend *The Proteas of Southern Africa*, 1980, by J. P. Rourke, Purnell, Capetown; *South Africa's Proteaceae*, 1982, by M. Vogt, Proteaflora Enterprises, Melbourne; *Proteas for Pleasure*, 1976, by S. Eliovson, Macmillan South Africa Publishers, Johannesburg; and *South African Proteaceae in New Zealand*, 1983, by L. J. Matthews, Matthews Publishing, Levin.

A rare white queen protea (*Protea magnifica*).

A regal floral rendering of a king's crown; this variety typifies king proteas *(Protea cynaroides)*. Most common in winter, it replaces the variety with rounded bracts encountered in the fall.

KING PROTEA
Protea cynaroides

Other Names: Giant protea

Exquisitely regal in size, color and symmetry, the king protea has been described as "possibly the most spectacular flower in the world." Prime flowerheads top 12" in diameter, although 6–7" is more typical.

Officially South Africa's national flower, the king, with its pointed, silvery-pink bracts ringing a central snowy, floral "mountain," is a visual delight. Each rosy bract is densely coated with white hairs, reminiscent of the silvery coating on Maui's native silverswords.

The earliest king illustration (1705) was inscribed "African tree-artichoke." How mundane, yet it inspired the scientific name which means "protea like a globe artichoke." In addition, a comparison of these two unrelated plants helps us understand the basic structure of protea blossoms (p.13).

Many Hawaiian floral arrangements and boxed proteas are designed around kings, whose several varieties, encompassing different flowering periods, make them available year-round.

King proteas play a rascally game with gardeners. Several times annually the 3–4' high bush sends out immense silvery-pink buds. Wonderful, one thinks. Much to the gardener's disappointment, however, these buds repeatedly turn into yet another set of green leaves. Eventually real flowerbuds appear which slowly unfurl their pink-silky majesty.

14

Bucketfuls of king proteas in various stages of maturation await shipment.

Magnificent king proteas grow on low bushes in Kula, Maui.

A rare white king is guaranteed to bring expressions of delight from everyone, including protea growers and handlers who see dozens of kings daily.

Clad in a layered woolly overcoat, this classic queen protea (*Protea magnifica*) lives up to its scientific name, "the magnificent protea."

QUEEN PROTEA
Protea magnifica (=barbigera)
Other Names: Giant woolly-beard,   woolly-headed protea

A fitting partner to the king, the dignified queen protea exudes sensual fluffiness. From fleecy buds, its rosy-red, fur-tipped bracts expand outward to reveal a woolly interior culminating in a black velvety knob.

Second largest of all proteas (the king is largest), its blooms (5–8″ across), vary in color from soft pink to watermelon red on one hand and from orange, creamy yellow (this form is presumed extinct in the wild) to clear green on the other. The fleecy trimmings typically mix white and gold.

Their attractive fuzziness is not purely ornamental. Nature designs animal and floral fur for practical reasons: warmth and protection from desiccation. Not surprisingly, the grandest queens are those from alpine habitats. Rugged environmental and climatic conditions—icy

This atypical variety of queen, chartreuse and gold, also thrives in the cold upcountry winters.

winds and snowy blizzards whipping across craggy mountaintops — have all contributed towards the evolution of these glorious flowerheads. After seeing thousands of these beauties, powdered with snow and sprawling across rocky slopes above Capetown, naturalist John Rourke likened them to "candied flowers atop monstrous sugar confections ...cloaked in an air of unreality" (1980). Having struggled for survival, queens are hardy, lasting up to 30 years in captivity. Cold weather is essential. Given warm, humid, poorly-drained or shaded locations they quickly harbor fatal fungal diseases.

Flowering primarily from October to May, queens grow well on Maui from 3,000' to 4,000' elevation. In Africa they occur up to 9,000'.

A close-up view of the queen protea's furry bracts.

Another infrequently encountered queen, this orange one has not yet opened fully. Most boxes and bouquets of proteas for export include queens, kings or both.

A little hesitant to open fully, the "princess protea" *(Protea grandiceps)* was an early favorite of the English aristocracy.

PRINCESS PROTEA
Protea grandiceps

Other Names: Peach or oval-leaved protea

Described as "breathtakingly arresting," the "princess" is aptly named. Her arching bracts, peach or coral-red, are fringed with long, feathery fringes that mimic silky eyelashes. She is even a little too shy to open fully. Her top is almost flat and partly encloses a mass of white plumose flowers.

The luxuriant fur coat of the "princess" indicates her alpine nature. At home on exposed talus slopes near Capetown, she is seldom seen out of cultivation except by robust mountaineers, as many populations have been destroyed by fires. She is one of the fussiest proteas, refusing to bloom or even dying if the weather becomes too wet or too warm. She hates to get her feet wet too, withering if the soil does not have just the right amount of rockiness and slope. Blooming months are winter and spring.

English protea aficionados in the early 19th Century were so captivated by the "princess" that they catered to her every whim. Noticing that even minute amounts of sun induced richer colors into her flowerheads, hobbyists trundled the large pot-plants in and out of greenhouses according to the vagaries of the weather. Anyone who has experienced the English climate can well assume that this was time-consuming. Were these English blooms as brilliant as the "princesses" from sunny Maui? Probably not, as with each passing year Hawaii's proteas exceed world standards for beauty, intensity of color, length of stem, and other important horticultural parameters.

The alpine preferences of the "princess" are reflected in her feathery attire.
Proteas, as well as people, need fur coats when it snows.

Resembling the "princess," the apple-green protea *(Protea coronata)* is a clear grass-green trimmed with white fleece. Its coloration darkens with age.

Silvery-pink bracts fringed with brown fur characterize Stokoe's protea *(Protea stokoei)*, a less common but most handsome species.

When backlit by the sun, the wineglass-shaped flowerheads of the "prince" glow with a rich translucency. The front cover photo on this book is also of a "prince protea."

PRINCE PROTEA
Protea compacta

Other Names: Bot River or pink protea, "pink lady," cv Pink Snow

When proteas were first grown by European royalty, a hobby which peaked around 1800, no one bothered with "marketable" names. Part of the snobbishness of cultivating these exotic blooms was knowing their botanical names. The "prince," a member of the newly created "Royal Family of Proteas," is an excellent example of a solution to naming difficulties facing marketing specialists in Hawaii. Neither its South African name, Bot River protea, nor its scientific name, *Protea compacta*, did justice to the shapely 4" x 4" flowerheads, whose rosy hue has been adopted as a fashion color, "protea pink," in Africa. Thus the name "prince" was invented.

Easy to grow, the "prince" is merely another beautiful species in Hawaii. In England it is especially popular and in Africa is grown in such quantity that thousands of seeds are broadcast over newly plowed land in the manner of sowing wheat.

Its season is November to May. Unfortunately, the leaves discolor within a few days of cutting. Snip them off and return the flower to your arrangement.

DUCHESS PROTEA
Protea eximia

Other Names: Ray-flowered protea,
cv "Rose-spoon," cv "Pink-spoon"

A large, reddish flowerhead characterized by shimmering, spoon-shaped bracts and a central mound of regal burgundy velvet, the "duchess" is at its peak of perfection just before fully opening. Within a few days it turns scraggly.

The scientific name *eximia* means "distinguished." Its noble appearance and ease of cultivation earned it early popularity among the European aristocracy. The velvet-knobbed flowers and fuzzy bracts of the "duchess" indicate its tolerance to cold and an ability to reflect harmful light rays. The natural habitat of this species is in the mountains above Capetown, South Africa, where crisp dry winds and icy nights have helped mold extensive shrublands.

This protea is unusual in that it roots from cuttings. It then grows so fast that horticulturalists recommend regular pinching-back to encourage branching. If conditions are optimal, the "duchess" will even bloom before two years of age. The season is November to May.

The "duchess" *(Protea eximia)* (above) is easily recognized by its spoon-shaped bracts, a characteristic which is retained even after hybridization (below).

Smaller than all the previous species, the common variety of "red baron" *(Protea obtusifolia)* has deep red bracts.

RED BARON
Protea obtusifolia

Other Names: Bredasdorp sugar-bush, "jester," cv Greenvalley White, cv Greenvalley Red

This compact species comes in red and green variants. Smooth and shiny, its bracts fit snugly against one another. It is one of the smaller proteas, resembling a partially opened sugarbush.

The "red baron" was not culti-vated until 1914, over 100 years after its relatives had become popular in Europe. An easy, fast grower, it is tolerant to a wide range of climatic and soil conditions, especially pH, blooming in less than eighteen months. Fairly long-lived, it is available from September to May.

The green form of "red baron" has a transparent texture that is typical of many members of the genus *Protea.*

PINK MINK
Protea neriifolia

Other Names: Oleander-leaved or bearded protea. Cultivars include "yellow mink," "white mink," and "green ice"

More than 350 years ago, an unknown Dutch mariner picked up a dried seedhead of this "graceful thistle" and carried it back to Europe, giving it the distinction of being both the first protea, and the first South African plant ever described. From these distant, humble beginnings the exciting eras of exploration, discovery, collecting, dissecting, describing, and illustrating proteas have ultimately led to growing, hybridizing, and commercial marketing of many species of proteas.

In their homeland, southern Africa, "minks" dot hillsides and bluffs from sea-level to 4,300' elevation. In some places extensive stands cover entire slopes.

Today, wherever it is grown, this silky protea, with sleek fur-tipped bracts and long narrow leaves, is a favorite. The many stunning varieties provide a blooming season from August to March. Each flowerhead is a deep cup 5" x 3", seldom opening wider. Up to 250 may be produced annually from a single bush. They grow easily and are very suitable for home gardens. Minks are included in almost all gift-packages originating in Hawaii and are often seen in Japanese *ikebana* or contemporary tropical flower arrangements.

Always a favorite, the large, elongated flowerheads of "pink mink" protea *(Protea neriifolia)* stimulate one's tactile senses.

A delicate, pale variant of "pink mink."

A "yellow mink," tipped with black fur; note how this differs from "yellow mink" on the title page of this section, which sports chestnut fur.

Note how the feathery-fringed bracts gently curve inwards at the top; this is about as open as a "pink mink" will get.

An unusual variant of "pink mink," accented with white fur, harmonizes several pastel colors.

Sold in Hawaii as "black mink," this longish, narrow, black-bearded protea
(Protea lepidocarpodendron) produces variable amounts of black, but is
always trimmed with black, velvety fur.

ERMINE TAIL
Protea longifolia

Other Names: Long-leaved protea

Protea growers in Hawaii changed the name of this charming species from long-leaved protea to "ermine tail."

One of the distinctive features of this exquisitely symmetrical protea is its fluffy white mass of flowers which culminates in a central "tail" of black velvet. Loosely enclosing this feathery mound are translucent, chartreuse bracts.

People tend to prefer the pink varieties of proteas but the "ermine tail" is different. Its pellucid lightness provides an elegant contrast in flower arrangements.

In the wild, the "ermine tail" has earned a reputation for promiscuity by hybridizing freely with nearby species. This "immorality," however, has never diminished its popularity. An early entrant to horticulture, it was growing in London by 1790 and soon thereafter became a favorite of Austrian royalty.

The spreading shrubs of this species, bearing many large, pale flowerheads (5–6″ long) average only 3′ high. Such profusion imparts a top-heaviness to the bushes. Unfortunately the "ermine tail" dies young. After taking four years to bloom, its energy fizzles around ten years of age. Blooms are available from December to May.

Growing with its flowerheads resting close to or on the ground, the ground rose *(Protea pudens)* resembles a miniature "ermine tail."

One of the characteristics of "ermine tail" is its fluffy, elongated "tail" of black velvet, which is retained during hybridization.

SUGARBUSH
Protea repens

Other Names: "Honey protea"

Sugarbush *(Protea repens)* originally covered such vast areas in South Africa that early Dutch settlers would pick them by the thousands, not to take home and keep in vases, but to collect their copious sweet nectar, which was then boiled down into a syrup. The flowers, incidentally, were tossed by the wayside.

With its proudly symmetrical, sticky, rose-and-cream flowerheads set amidst narrow, leathery leaves, the sugarbush is one of Hawaii's prettiest and historically interesting ornamental proteas.

They once grew so plentifully that sailors rounding the Cape of Good Hope in the 16th Century picked basketloads of flowers with which to sweeten foods. The floral equivalent of the mainland's sugar maple or the Pacific's coconut palm, sugarbush's honeyed nectar was eagerly and extensively exploited until 1900. Both rural and urban residents spent whole days picking flowers, shaking their sugary globules into earthenware jars then boiling the liquid down to produce a thick syrup. An essential item in every kitchen and medicine chest for over a century, this "bush syrup" was immortalized in folksong and featured regularly in agricultural shows and big county fairs. Today only one bottle is known — an 1890s museum piece.

It is said that while Empress Josephine's husband, Napoleon, was busy warring in Europe, she was passing the time with her favorite hobby, tending sugarbushes and other proteas!

Given the sugarbush's abundance and hardiness in its native country, it comes as no surprise that its distinctions include being the first protea to bloom outside Africa, and the first to become established in overseas gardens such as California, Australia, and New Zealand. A latecomer to Hawaii in the 1960s, it blooms year-round, peaking in summer; it is reliable, adaptable, and may live as long as 30 years. Try tasting its fresh, sweet nectar — the Japanese White-eyes (tiny green birds, *Zosterops japonicus*) and ants love it too.

An unusual pale variety of sugarbush.

BABY PROTEAS
Protea aurea (=longifolia),
P. mundii, P. lacticolor, P. punctata

Other Names: "Candelites," "candlesticks," "mini-proteas"

Long-bud protea *(Protea aurea)* bursts open overnight into pink floral fireworks.

This charming assemblage of protea cousins enhances bouquets with its slim buds and dainty, widely opening flowers. Special beauty comes from the fresh glowing colors (pink, cream, green, or rose).

Most proteas do not open indoors unless they have already begun to expand on the bush. Baby proteas are different. They are customarily picked in tight bud from which they open overnight. One pays for this privilege, though, by their short vase-life—about one week.

Mund's protea (*P. mundii* cv Jack Clark), of reddish rather than pink hue, begins life as a candle-like bud, then quickly unfolds its richness. This species is so tolerant of the sun, so sturdy, and such a rapid grower that in South Africa it is used to pioneer deforested lands in preparation for reestablishing native coastal shrublands. In Hawaii, some farms use it as breeding stock.

Baby protea (*P. lacticolor*), whether in its white ("snow dove") or pink ("baby pink") forms, exhibits a charming daintiness.

BLUSHING BRIDE
Serruria florida

How fortunate we are to have this charming little protea in Hawaii, even if it is somewhat rare here!

The blushing bride's nodding, creamy flowerheads are delicately flushed with pink flecks, while on the inside is a mass of silky pink fluff. Flowers worn in buttonholes by courting young men evidently gave rise to the common name. Its long vase-life is well-known, and in Africa it is also occasionally used in wedding bouquets.

This unusual protea has a history that is typical of endangered plants. It was never abundant, being restricted to one small mountainous area in South Africa. After its discovery in 1773, the entire species was lost until 1891! When rediscovered, this little treasure was given every means of protection, even to the extent of guarding the few captive plants. However, protecting it in the wild has presented a conservation dilemma: man-made fires have destroyed most of the few remaining plants, yet in nature, the seeds germinate only after a veld fire burns through an area.

Even the names of the blushing bride's sole habitat, Assegaaiboskloof, in the steep granitic Franschhoek Mts., where mist clouds habitually blanket the mountaintops, lend an aura of mystery to this delicate charmer.

Despite a tenuous natural existence, bushes of the blushing bride perform quite well in cultivation but, alas, last not much longer than brides blush — about three years. In Hawaii, you might be lucky to encounter them from October to February.

Subtly flecked with rosy "blushes," this dainty cream protea is practically extinct in its natural haunts.

PINCUSHIONS

Bright red "ribbons" resemble tongues of fire bursting from Africa's bushlands: a mass of Veldfire pincushions.

SUNBURST
Leucospermum cordifolium

Other Names: Nodding pincushion, "Hawaiian sunburst." Cultivars and hybrids include "firefly," "firewheel," "cloudbank" and "eldorado." Similar species: narrow-leaved pincushion, "galaxy," "lime pin" or "tangerine pin" *(L. lineare)* and "orange flame" *(L. vestitum)*

A richly glowing "Hawaiian sunburst" *(Leucospermum cordifolium)*, the most common, well-known, abundant, and cheapest protea grown in Hawaii, is most prolific during winter and spring.

One of the first proteas to be described and drawn, around 1700, the first protea to be termed "pincushion," and the first to be grown in quantity outside Africa, the "sunburst" is the best known of all proteas. Its dome-shaped, orange, red, pink, or yellow flowerhead, 3–4" across, begins life covered with glossy loops. Each loop, a modified flower, springs outwards as it matures. When all loops have sprung, the overall effect is like a burst of orange fireworks.

The "sunburst's" elegant flower-heads, with their conspicuous "pins" —"butterfly feelers" if you like—are difficult to figure out. Many people ask, "Are they real?" For those interested in the botanical makeup, the curved "pins" are female parts (styles) and the "ribbons" are composed of male parts (anthers, stamens) fused with perianth segments (petals plus sepals).

Generally blooming in their first year, their low bushes produce bountifully, averaging about 250 blooms annually. Conditions on Maui are so excellent that in 1978 a 14-year-old plant budded off 1,200 flowerheads. For the home-gardener, planting is recommended every five years. The optimum flowering period is December through March, which conveniently fits into the California March-to-May and South African September-to-November seasons. Hawaii is thus assured an important slot in the world market, as its peak season not only fills an international gap but coincides with Christmas, New Year, Valentine's Day and can even stretch to Easter.

On Maui, sturdy "coffin boxes" of pincushions and other proteas,

"Sunbursts," glowing.

A yellow-orange form of "Hawaiian sunburst" is known as "carnival" because of the different colors produced on its bush by young, mature, and old blooms.

wrapped individually in tissue paper, are airfreighted daily to foreign cities such as Tokyo and Amsterdam as well as all over the United States. Real "jet-set globe-trotters," they not only delight their recipients but win prizes in inter-national flower shows, competing with exotic orchids, world-class roses, and famous Dutch daffodils.

Pincushions are the only proteas fashioned into leis. On notable civic occasions it is not unusual to see prominent citizens draped with garlands of these floral fireworks. Given refrigeration, such a lei lasts one month.

The vibrant colors, stiff glossi-ness, lasting qualities, and fanciful appearance of the "sunburst" all combine to create a dramatic cut flower. Combine them with other proteas, gingers, heliconias, or tropical foilage to create stunning flower arrangements, large or small.

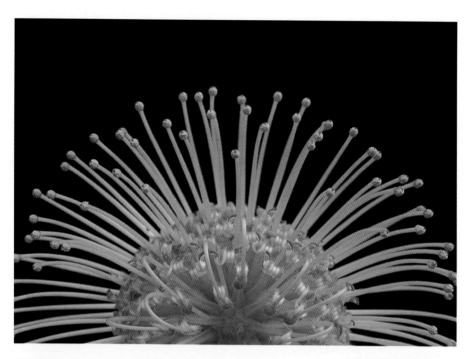

"Firefly" pincushion, a hybrid between "Hawaiian sunburst" and "pink star;" whether in a half-circle or as twins, they resemble brightly-rayed suns.

PINK STAR
Leucospermum tottum

Other Names: Firewheel or spreading pincushion, "cinnamon pin," "Maui sunset"

"Pink star" *(Leucospermum tottum),* a finer and more delicate flower than the "sunburst," is not abundant, yet even a single flowerhead enhances a bouquet.

The daintiest of pincushion proteas, "pink star" is one of my favorites. Its graceful flowerheads (3–4" diameter) resemble symmetrically curving domes which change color and size with age. Each downy pink flowerbud (a single loop) splits into two parts: a rolled-up "ribbon" and glossy-tipped "pin," as in all pincushions. In a few days the flowerheads darken so much that they have been mistaken for different species.

"Pink star's" bushes, only about 3' high, are perfect for upcountry gardeners. Neatly rounded, they produce a plethora of charming, long-stemmed flowerheads which suit many different styles of flower arranging. The bush requires little care and produces most of the year but particularly during winter. It is worth growing them just to receive warm smiles from your friends as you give them bouquets.

PINWHEEL
Leucospermum catherinae

Other Names: Catherine's Pinwheel, catherine wheel leucospermum, "combflower"

The pinwheel's loops (styles) recoil outwards like a catherine wheel, exposing their "hot" cerise tips. Is it a pink-footed floral centipede spinning cartwheels across the page?

Largest and most novel of the pincushions, the "pinwheel" begins life relatively small (2½" diameter in bud), yellow, and covered with about 140 loops. This is most likely how you will see it in a giftbox or while visiting a protea farm. Over the next few days the loops flick outwards exposing their cerise tips. When all 5 or 6 circles of loops have recoiled, their tips bent sideways in the same direction, the entire effect is of a multiple-layered, gold and pink pinwheel, 5–6" in diameter.

The scientific name, *Leucospermum catherinae,* refers both to this spinning "catherine-wheel" effect and to Catherine van der Byl, a South African who was instrumental in determining the species' natural distribution.

The "pinwheel's" robust shrub grows easily, reaching about 6' in height, but its flowers are not as prolific as the common "sunburst" or "pink star." They are available in limited quantity during Hawaii's cooler months.

HAWAII GOLD*

Leucospermum cv Hawaii Gold

The first hybrid released from the University of Hawaii's Agricultural Experiment Station in Kula, Maui (the world's leading center for protea research), Hawaii Gold is thought to be a natural hybrid of two South African pincushions (*L. cuneiforme* and *L. conocarpodendron*). It has an unusual history. Although the seeds came from an *L. cuneiforme* nursery plant, many aspects of its growth, shape, and size did not match that of the parent. In 1973, protea specialist Dr. Parvin took detailed descriptions and photographs of this atypical plant to South Africa, where it was agreed that this was a natural hybrid in which pollen from a *L. conocarpodendron* plant had

---

*Hawaii Gold is the sole, internationally accepted, common name for this cultivar.

somehow been deposited (perhaps by a sunbird) on the receptive female portion of *L. cuneiforme*. Thus a unique pincushion had been formed, having rich golden flowers with furry, curly centers. It is similar to Veldfire but, instead of fiery streaks, has pure gold.

Beginning in February, Hawaii Gold blooms quite prolifically for several months. Like other pincushions, it reproduces well from grafts and cuttings (which is why that first plant now has so many offspring). The cut flower shrivels when dried.

The brilliant gold loopings of a prime Hawaii Gold hybrid are particularly special to islanders, as this pincushion was the first hybrid released from the Kula Agricultural Experiment Station on Maui, the world's center for protea research.

VELDFIRE
Leucospermum cv Veldfire

With orange, red, and gold streaks nestled in and bursting forth from a dome of white fluffiness, Veldfire is well named. Another natural hybrid pincushion from South Africa, its vibrant colors recall the intensity of raging fires on a veld (savannah).

As with other pincushions, Veldfire's cut flowers are available from fall to spring, lasting about three weeks when picked fresh. Though stiffish, they do not dry well.

This particular variety was brought to Maui by Dr. Philip Parvin in the early 1970s as part of Maui's floriculture trade. At the Kula Agricultural Research Center, ongoing research touches many phases of protea biology: propagation, habitat requirements, hybridization, and diseases. Dazzling beauties such as Veldfire will undoubtedly continue to delight Hawaii residents and visitors, and reach out through giftboxes to many who have not yet visited the islands.

Veldfire pincushion, a hybrid from South Africa, can scarcely be rivaled in intensity of color. Its tongues of bright colors—yellow, orange, and red—evoke images of blazing grass fires on Africa's velds.

A bouquet of pincushions—pinwheels, Hawaii Golds, "Hawaiian sunbursts," "fireflies," Veldfires and hybrids. Pincushions hybridize more freely than other members of the protea family, and therefore exhibit the most variety.

LEUCADENDRONS
(FOLIAGE PROTEAS)

A particularly stunning male cone of "flametip."

SILVER TREE
Leucadendron argenteum

Male cones and leaves of the silver tree *(Leucadendron argenteum)*, grown for ornament and foliage rather than for flowers.

With its silvery, silken leaves glistening in the sunlight, this landscaping gem may be seen year-round in Maui's upcountry gardens and protea farms. It is especially lovely when gentle breezes ruffle its foliage.

As with Haleakala's silversword (they are unrelated), the silver tree's leaves are densely coated with long white hairs which reflect harmful light rays away and prevent excessive moisture loss. This is particularly important for plants living in exposed, arid places. The silver tree comes from a habitat similar to California chaparral near Capetown, South Africa.

Their lustrous, satiny leaves are long-lasting and so popular that the few remaining wild stands have recently been protected from the traditional tourist practice of cutting leaves for souvenir bookmarks. In early colonial days, this gorgeous tree was (good gracious!) commonly cut for fuel and construction.

The silver tree is attractive right from the sapling stage (pinch back to encourage low branching if you own one) through to a mature 25-foot-high tree. Watch out though: It is temperamental. In both wild and cultivated situations, the silver tree may suddenly and mysteriously wither away. Fungi and soil nematodes are the usual culprits.

Silver trees come in two sexes, the same as you and I — male and female. Both bear reproductive structures resembling silver pinecones. The female cone, which remains closed, is largest and prettiest.

Upright branches of the silver tree. Cones of both sexes are borne on the same tree. In mid-center is a female cone — taller and more closed than the male cone. How their leaves shimmer on breezy, sunshiny upcountry days!

FLAMETIP (male),
YELLOW TULIP (female)
Leucadendron discolor

Other Names: Sunshine bush, flame gold-tips

A gaudy bunch of "flametip" male cones in various stages of opening.

Available during winter and spring, "flametip" enhances protea bouquets and provides bright landscaping. These cheery, spreading bushes (up to 4 feet high) are topped with tulip-like flowerheads, rich creamy-gold with scarlet centers. They thrive in many types of soil and when in their native habitat are said to resemble "hills of sunshine."

All foliage proteas possess colored leaves surrounding pinecone-like centers. They are so variable that in South Africa people do not distinguish between the different species; they are all "cape greens," whose color, like fish, changes with season, age, and sex. "Flametip," with its distinct sexual dimorphism, provides a perfect example of why protea growers and florists prefer to use scientific instead of common names. In this species *(L. discolor),* only the *male* has the red center and is sold as "flametip." The *female,* with a small green center, is marketed as "yellow tulip," which would be fine if it were not the common name applied to the next species, *L. laureolum!*

YELLOW TULIP
Leucadendron laureolum

Foliage proteas look best *en masse*. No wonder the South Africans called this species one of the "sunshine bushes!"

Similar to "flametip" females (see p. 50), this protea is all-yellow. Its floral foliage is a dazzling sight in winter and spring, when both sexes of cones become surrounded by longish, rather fancy, lemon-colored leaves.

In upcountry areas of Hawaii, winters bring "cold" weather (down to the high 30°s F). Residents pull out their "winter woollies," many shrubs and trees suspend flowering, and storms interrupt bouts of fine weather. It is at these times that "yellow tulips," "flametips," Safari Sunsets, and other attractive foliage-proteas intensify their gay colors.

Bright flashes of yellow typify the "yellow tulip," a popular foliage protea that is added to bouquets as a "filler."

An attractive foliage protea, *Leucadendron rubrum.*

Miscellaneous foliage proteas; those with closed cones are the female *multicones,* and those with more widely opening cones are the male *multifloras.* Their foliage is often feathery.

SAFARI SUNSET, SILVAN RED

Leucadendron hybrids

Bright red or orange-red terminal leaves typify this Safari Sunset, a popular hybrid developed "down-under." Note the fine fuzz edging each colored leaf.

These new, red-foliaged hybrids from Australian and New Zealand horticulturalists are popular in Hawaii as bouquet-fillers and for garden color during the cooler months. Exported worldwide, they are currently considered the most significant of "down-under-raised" leucadendrons. Unlike the yellow-foliaged proteas, whose bushes are low and bear upright stems terminating in ornamental leaves, these hybrids may grow 8–10' high if not pruned annually.

Their bright leaves (bracts) are usually mistaken for flowers. Look at the "petals" closely. They have the same shape as the green leaves below them, but are colored and more clustered. Safari Sunset's true petals, huddling together to form the cone inside its red leaves, are unrecognizable. Simple proteas like this help us appreciate the elaborate specialization of larger proteas such as the king and queen. These latter represent a high stage of floral evolution in which the terminal leaves on a stem have metamorphosed into layers of elegant, fur-trimmed bracts that mimic flower petals even more closely than do the colored leaves of foliage proteas.

BANKSIAS

Ashby's banksia *(Banksia ashbyi)* is perhaps unique among all plants in that its large pollen-laden flower-spikes smell like buttered popcorn. Real butter, that is, not margarine.

A WORD ABOUT BANKSIAS

Hill banksia *(Banksia collina)* is a pretty and prolific shrub but its flowers seem to resist growing long stems; thus it is not often seen in bouquets.

Banksias, although occurring in myriad colors and sizes, all share a sameness which, like hibiscus, makes them instantly recognizable even to laymen.

Most obvious are their dense cylindrical (sometimes conical), spiky flowerheads which exhibit spiral, ribbed, or coiled patterns. Many resemble corn cobs. Imagine one. Instead of the rounded kernels, substitute hundreds of narrow colored tubes projecting outwards. Each tube, representing one flower, is at first looped but eventually splits into two parts: a yellow male portion and a spiky, knobbed female portion. These split flowers form the yellow bands that are so characteristic of banksias. Banksia flowerheads—each is composed of numerous individual flowers—are so complex that if you cannot figure them out do not feel that you are lacking in intelligence; just enjoy their beauty.

All 73 species occur naturally in Australia, their sole country of origin. Most are from the southwestern deserts, to which they are cleverly adapted to deal with temperature extremes and scarcity of water. Rugged, leathery evergreens, their rough, durable qualities enable them to keep well whether in or out of water, fresh or dried.

Approximately 20 species of banksias grow on the slopes of Haleakala, Maui; none are hybrids. Winter months provide the most floral diversity.

WOOLLY BANKSIA
Banksia baueri

Other Names: Possum or woolly- spiked banksia

Largest of all banksias, the woolly *(Banksia baueri)* commonly attains 10″ in length and 6″ in diameter. Its trio of hues—fawn, tan, and lime-green—produce an unusual combination.

Without question my favorite banksia, this huge, curly, furry delight must be seen to be appreciated. Anything it lacks in bright colors is amply compensated for by its personality (especially when two eyes are added). Its sheer size alone is impressive. Largest of all banksias,

its flowerhead commonly reaches 10 inches long by 6 inches wide. Colors range from subtle mauvish-gray to bright tan (especially when young), with yellow-green on the inside.

Its fuzzy nature is a telltale sign of its natural habitat: desert. Native to sandy, barren scrublands of the

Nullabor Plain (one of the harshest deserts in the world), the woolly banksia's fluffy overcoat protects both its flowers and seeds from desiccation during the scorching days and keeps it warm through frosty nights. It is not surprising that in Australia the flower spikes emerge only during winter and spring, thus avoiding excessive heat. In Hawaii, where temperature extremes are less marked, the season is summer and fall.

The woolly banksia grows easily in Maui, although only a few farms carry it. Curiously, its enormous flowers are borne not on tall shrubs but from low, sprawling bushes.

As these curious botanical novelties wither, their long "fur" turns shaggy, inspiring creative artists to transform them into cute toys.

"Woolly buddies," creations of Ehu Farm, Maui, come in a multitude of personalities from elephants to "Care Bears."

SUMMER LIME
Banksia baxteri

Other Names: Bird's nest or Baxter's banksia, "lime green" or "green banksia"

"Summer lime" *(Banksia baxteri)* is a furry, desert-adapted banksia. Note how its leathery, rickracked leaves appear to have been chopped off at their tips.

With its yellow-green flower spikes shaped like flattened acorns, this fall species is decorative and long-lasting, equally at home in fresh or dried flower arrangements.

Also from the Nullabor Plain in Western Australia, this species takes no chances with sunburning and desiccation. Nature has provided it with a variety of heat-protective devices: silky structures to enclose flower- and leaf-buds, dense woolli-ness on young stems, furry overcoats for its numerous flowers, fuzziness all over its prickly waxy leaves, and even thickly coated seed-capsules.

As you drive, wearing sunglasses, up the steep driveways of banksia farms on the slopes of Haleakala, it is easy to appreciate the fact that this banksia thrives with bright sun-shine beaming down on well-drained slopes. It dies if these conditions are not met.

GOLDEN ACORN
Banksia burdettii

Other Names: Burdett's banksia, "golden banksia"

Appropriately named, the "golden acorn" bursts with brilliantly colored pollen. Its shape is always shorter and more compact than its close relative "orange frost."

A downy, golden banksia similar to but smaller than "orange frost," "golden acorn" is a popular fall addition to protea bouquets.

Plants from dry, windy, and alpine habitats tend to have furry or waxy coverings; this is nature's way of conserving water. In banksias, the hairs are short but dense enough to allow survival in the notoriously scorching climate which occurs over more than half of the Australian continent. The knobbed white coatings of "golden acorn" and "orange frost" banksias are especially noticeable in bud. Their leaves and stems are also covered with fine fuzz and/or wax.

"Golden acorn" was a relatively late discovery (1930). Its natural geographic range is narrow and less than 30 miles long. Despite this rarity, its beautiful golden blooms (3½–5" long) are still exploited commercially in Australia. Bushfires too have taken their toll. It is fortunate that it thrives so well in Hawaii. In future years, the islands may well be the major source of cuttings for other countries experimenting in protea/banksia farming.

"Golden acorn" banksia.

SCARLET BANKSIA
Banksia coccinea

Other Names: Waratah banksia, Albany banksia, "kahili"

Neat vertical rows of "crocheted" red and white loops characterize the scarlet banksia, one of the least common species in Hawaii. Its scientific name is appropriate: *coccinea* is Latin for scarlet.

Also from Western Australia, scarlet banksia is less desert-adapted than most of the other banksias treated in this book, preferring relatively moist, shaded locations within scrublands. It will develop into a 25-foot-high tree if conditions are right. Like its relatives, it is pollinated in Hawaii by bees.

Stiffly stitched loops in rows of red and white, making up the scarlet banksia's flowers *(Banksia coccinea)*, almost look as though man's handiwork contributed to its construction. Each loop will eventually flick outwards.

RASPBERRY FROST
Banksia menziesii

Other Names: Menzies' or firewood banksia, "burgundy," "pink frost" or "frosted white banksia"

Banksias differ from many plants and animals in that their youth is not the most physically beautiful phase! During middle age, banksias such as "raspberry frost" gleam with depth of color and symmetry. This species was named after Archibald Menzies, a noted Pacific naturalist.

A close-up of "raspberry frost," showing the intricate colors within the flowerhead's vertical columns of individual flowers. Each tube, at first looped, eventually splits into two parts: a yellow male portion, and a spiky, knobbed female portion.

One of the prettiest banksias, this one is burgundy with vertical, silvery stripes. As it matures, ever-widening bands of bright yellow appear from below. This is due to the individual spiky flowers opening up and exposing pollen. "Raspberry frost" retains its colors fairly well when dried, adding variety to the predominant yellows and greens of other dry species.

One of the taller shrubs, growing up to 30' high, "raspberry frost" produces up to 60 blooms per plant each year, primarily during summer and fall. It is a special favorite of ants, who love its nectar, causing headaches to protea packers.

"Raspberry frost" thrives, as do most banksias, in sunny weather and well-drained soils. Its tough, finely fuzzy leaves are serrated and crinkly. It is also fire-tolerant. Such qualities spell ruggedness and resilience. Armed with extremely thick bark and a woody underground stem, the bush can sprout anew after raging fires, relatively common occurrences (natural or man-induced) in Australia's shrublands.

Both its scientific and Australian common names commemorate Archibald Menzies, the noted surgeon-naturalist on Vancouver's expedition to the Pacific during the late 18th Century. Menzies is of special interest as he was an important plant-collector in both Australia and Hawaii. Today several native Hawaiian plants (including a treefern) are named after him. And now thousands of people worldwide can also enjoy his Australian namesake and recent import, this lovely burgundy and yellow banksia.

A mass of red and white stripes — scarlet and "raspberry frost" banksias. Who knows where they will eventually bring joy to people — Chicago, Atlanta, Paris, or perhaps Tokyo?

INDIAN SUMMER
Banksia occidentalis

Other Names: Red swamp banksia, water bush, "red banksia"

"Indian summer's" ruby-red flower spikes, set amidst softish, narrow leaves, look like looped bottlebrushes. Note the creamy green color inside the red curls.

This is not a desert plant, hence it is not as prickly and woolly as most other banksias. On Maui, birds such as the Japanese White-eye *(mejiro)* and house finch feed on insects in its shrubby foliage and sometimes even nest there. Its preference for marshes is reflected in its Australian names above.

"Indian summer" grows and blooms easily in Hawaii, although this is not always true elsewhere. Hawaii's combination of climate, soil, water regime, cloud patterns, and natural drainage, although not exactly equivalent to the small area in Western Australia where it is native, appears to be ideal. It flowers during fall and spring. Blooms are best when fresh.

Two fine specimens of "Indian summer" *(Banksia occidentalis)*, a bottlebrush-like banksia from Western Australia.

RICKRACK BANKSIA

Banksia speciosa

Other Names: Showy or green banksia, "mint julep"

No one would want to sew these rickracks on a dress — they are too stiff and prickly. But their durable qualities enable them to last, with barely a water change, for a couple of months.

Spiralled rows of chartreuse spikes topped by woolly caps characterize this large-flowered banksia. Adding to the dramatic flair are its long, arching, "rickracked" leaves. Because it hails from arid terrain, its prickly foliage and durable flower-heads retain their freshness even after days without water and thousands of miles of airplane travel. An adaptable grower, it requires little attention and flourishes all-year in home gardens. The major flowering period is summer and fall.

Stiffly elegant, even one of its greenish flowerheads in a vase is sufficient. The "rickrack banksia" also dresses up baskets, wreaths, bouquets, gift-boxes or elaborate flower arrangements. The Australian name, showy banksia, reiterates the scientific name *speciosa* or "showy."

"Rickrack banksia" displays a different type of fire-resistance than "raspberry frost." Here, an intense fire kills the bush but not its stony seed-capsules which may sit dormant for years. Eventually, even a light spattering of rain is sufficient to nudge its safely ensconced seeds to life.

A close-up of "orange frost." The dense woolly coverings protect the banksia's flowerbuds from drying out.

ORANGE FROST
Banksia prionotes

Other Names: Orange or acorn banksia, "golden banksia"

Similar to "golden acorn," "orange frost" has longer flowerheads. How neatly arranged are its furry orange spirals of unopened flowers! The saffron band at the base is due to hundreds of individual flowers that are splitting open to expose their pollen.

This West Australian beauty bears abundant flower spikes that mimic big (5–6") acorns. Its compact, white, woolly buds open slowly to expose an ever-enlarging basal band of brilliant saffron. This bright color comes from the pollen.

Reaching 30' in height, "orange frost" bushes bear up to 60 blooms per year from March to December. Its long, leathery, saw-toothed leaves are well-named from the Greek roots *prion* (a saw) and *otes* (leaf margins).

In its semi-arid native habitat, certain curve-billed Australian honeyeaters poke between the pollen-laden flower spikes to sip nectar. On Maui, one of "orange frost's" new homes, similar birds, Hawaiian honeycreepers, are beginning to utilize this localized source of energy. Flying miles from mountain forests, Hawaii's native Apapanes *(Himatione sanguinea)* now visit banksia farms regularly.

This species provides another interesting example of name-changing. Inspired by the marketing success of "raspberry frost" (formerly Menzies' banksia), Hawaii protea growers discussed the idea of "orange frost" for the acorn banksia. Sales increased dramatically when this new commercial name hit the public eye!

AUSTRALIAN GOLDEN DRYANDRA
Dryandra formosa
Other Names: Showy dryandra, "golden emperor"

Though strictly speaking not a banksia, the Australian golden dryandra *(Dryandra formosa)* is a close relative. Note the deep golden fur atop its globular flowerhead. Both flowers and foliage dry well.

Named in honor of Jonas Dryandes, an 18th Century Swedish botanist who specialized in Australian plants, the dryandras are less woody than banksias though are obviously related to them. They even smell similar.

Note the dryandra's tight, globular flowerhead; those of banksias are more cylindrical. Its silvery interior and golden "fur," peaking on the upper surface, also recalls the true proteas from South Africa.

In Hawaii, the Australian golden dryandra's foliage is used more than the flowerheads. Its narrow, stiff-ribbed, serrated leaves—almost dainty—provide excellent filler material for dried wreaths, baskets, etc. Foliage is available year-round while flowerheads only occur during winter and spring.

CARE OF CUT FLOWERS

In addition to their beauty and charm, proteas have wonderfully long vase-lives. When properly handled some species will last four weeks or longer. It is easy to carry fresh flowers with you on your homebound airplane, or have them air-mailed. So long as no dirt is attached to the stems they will pass agricultural inspection at the airport. Most will survive 3–5 days without water, although obviously the sooner they receive water, the better.

If you receive a direct shipment from Hawaii, cut the woody stems with garden clippers or a sharp knife before placing them in water or a preservative solution. To enjoy your proteas and banksias for a maximum amount of time:
1. Change the water every few days.

Add more water every day for the first 2 or 3 days after receiving a gift-box, as the flowers will be thirsty.
2. Preservative solutions, available from some growers and florists, more than double vase life span.
3. Do not place in direct sun, near heaters, etc. Cool locations are best.
4. For extra months (or years) of pleasure from your flowers, you can dry or treat them with glycerine (see next section).

To order fresh or dried proteas/ banksias, contact any of the organizations mentioned in the "Acknowledgements" section of this book, (p. 5). Retail outlets such as The Protea Gift Shoppe, Maui Plantations, or florist shops are listed in the phone directory. Tourist and airline publications also regularly carry protea advertisements.

Buckets of proteas, picked during early morning hours, adorn benches at Maui Sunburst farm.

A typical mail-ordered box of mixed members of the protea family. The first peek at these stunning, unconventional flowers always elicits a joyful gasp.

The Protea Cooperative truck, a familiar sight around Kula's secondary roads, busily transfers fresh flowers from private farms to centralized buildings. Some farms utilize the cooperative method of pooling resources; others prefer the private business approach. Certain farms (for example, Protea Gardens of Maui and Olinda Vista Nursery) sell protea plants as well as flowers. Others (for example, Ehu Farm and Proteas of Hawaii) specialize in dried wreaths. All farms carry very high quality flowers. Each is checked for many types of flaws. If it fails the tests it is tossed into a large trash container or its bracts are twisted off and the patterned "floral skeleton" used for a dried specialty.

FLOWER ARRANGEMENT

Arranging flowers is like playing music, painting or performing any craft or inspirational activity. A mysterious energy stirs us from within, inducing a flow of immensely satisfying creativity.

Proteas in general possess heavy stems and large flowers. You cannot merely stick them in a jar and expect them to look like an arrangement in a fashion magazine. Flower arranging is not hard; it just takes a few materials and a modicum of concentration. Most people have an individual sense of proportion and color balance in relation to clothing and makeup (two other temporary creative arts), a talent which can easily be applied to flowers. Anyone can create a conversation-piece with fresh flowers, foliage, and the following items:

1. *Frogs.* These closely packed metal spikes attached to a heavy, solid base, are indispensable. *Heavy-duty floral foam* may also be used, although it breaks apart after one or two uses. An initial investment of "frogs" will last a lifetime. Buy several sizes (up to five inches in diameter) from a florist or garden supply store. Shop first by phone; "frogs" are not always available (especially in Hawaii). Homemade substitutes can be constructed from plywood and turned-up nails, using rocks as stabilizers. Short, sturdy sticks placed in the "frog" around a thick stem will hold it in place, especially if the stem is leaning. This technique is used extensively in Japan.

2. *Strong garden clippers* or *sharp knife.* Buy the clippers from a garden shop, drug- or dimestore. Every few days, recut the stems at an angle, preferably underwater. This allows water to pass more freely upwards. Trim off foliage that droops or interferes with the design. Do not squeeze the plant tissues any more than necessary.

3. *Vases.* Big, small, tall, flat and wide, round, square... invest in whatever you can afford. Experiment with casserole dishes, mixing bowls, spray-painted cake pans, wine bottles wound and glued with string, aluminum washing basins — whatever is appropriate. Vases with narrow tops do not work for thick-stemmed flowers and foliage. Japanese import shops and contemporary pottery outlets usually have shapely containers. Make sure your vases are scrupulously clean: wash out scum from previous flowers. Change water often.

4. Miscellaneous embellishments for hiding the "frog" and lower stems: *driftwood, river or beach stones* of various sizes, crinkly *lava rocks* (not from Hawaii's National Parks, where Pele, Hawaii's goddess of fire, may inflict calamity on you!), eroded *beach coral,* etc. A small supply of dried grasses, twisted vine stems, figurines, attractive seed-pods, etc., are additional options for creating different textural contrasts, moods, and "fillers."

Styles and Ideas

Each combination of flowers and foliage presents a unique challenge to the arranger. No one way is "right." Some favor splashes of vivid color that dazzle the eye. The more you add, the better. Strive for symmetry.

Flower arrangements combining proteas, heliconias, gingers, bromeliads, orchids, or other tropical foliage, decorate the spacious lobbies of most of Maui's deluxe hotels.

The oriental tradition in Hawaii leans towards modernization of traditional *ikebana* (Japanese flower arrangement) techniques: sleek, graphic and simple. Here, each element is trimmed and placed to reveal it as cleanly and favorably as possible. Every shape or geometric pattern is savored individually. The three basic lines are cut proportionately: *Select an appropriate length for the tallest stem* in proportion to the size of the container and amount of space the final arrangement will occupy, then *cut the middle stem two-thirds of that length,* and *the smallest stem one-half or one-third the length of the tallest stem.* Large proteas and banksias are ideal for these principal lines. Conventional flowers, smaller exotics, and foliage can then be added last. Favor asymmetry, simplicity and elegance. Do not clutter.

You can also try the "in-between" route, prevalent in many gorgeous arrangements found in hotels. Trailing orchids, large proteas and tropical foliage are topped by hanging heliconias or ornamental bananas. Such exotic elegance intermingles western, eastern and contemporary art. Many of the businesses that mail-order proteas also carry heliconias, gingers, calatheas, tropical foliage, anthuriums and orchids. (See *Tropicals: Heliconias, Gingers and Anthuriums in Hawaii,* by Kepler and Mau.)

Specific Examples
Intermingle proteas with temperate flowers: The splendid flowerheads of proteas combine well with the delicate, curved, or lacy nature of garden flowers such as poppies, feather cockscomb,

petunias, marigolds, daisies, asters and small-leaved foliage clipped from hedges or azaleas.

Don't neglect wild foliage: Snip off maple branches, dogwood sprays, trailing wild grape vines, goldenrods, pine branches or other seasonal foliage growing in your garden or along the roadside. Extra leaves trimmed from king proteas, silver tree and golden dryandra are especially useful and long-lasting.

Combine contrasts of texture and form: Fuzzy with smooth, lightness with heaviness, pointed with rounded, delicate with heavy, tall with fat, etc. Pink minks with sweet peas; banksias with petunias or carnations; multicones and multi-floras with the larger proteas; minks, queens and ermine tail with velvety tropical leaves.

Match textures and form: Pampas grass or papyrus with queens, big tropical leaves (monstera, variegated taro, etc.) with large protea flowerheads.

Combine tall, thin elements with low, round, thick ones: Gladioli with kings, queens and minks; long-stemmed lilies with prince proteas; snapdragons with Veldfire pin-cushions and foliage proteas.

Blend variegated foliage with solid colors: Multicolored *ti* leaves with prince or red baron; tricolor dracaena with duchess protea, sugar bush, and scarlet or golden acorn banksias.

Choose complementary colors, especially if the style is simple: Apple-green protea, ermine tail or pale varieties of sugarbush and red baron, with pink proteas and banksia.

Color coordinate for festive occasions: Blushing bride, babies' breath and ferns (wedding); princess, red baron and queen proteas with pine branches and silver pinecones (Christmas); anthuriums or red lobster claw heliconias, Safari Sunset foliage protea and heart-shaped philodendron leaves (Valentine's Day); golden queen, rockets, pincushions, orange frost, golden dryandra and yellow tulip foliage protea (golden anniversary); silver tree, white queen protea, white carnations, white calatheas (silver anniversary).

People who work with flowers are generally happy, personable, and gentle. In this very feminine photo-graph, an employee of Ehu Farm (Kula, Maui) picks queen, "prince," and duchess proteas to take to the large Protea Cooperative for sale and export.

DRIED PROTEAS AND BANKSIAS

Baskets and wreaths, hand-made and one-of-a-kind, are a lovely way to keep proteas for years. Only the choicest blossoms are used which, with controlled drying, retain their colors well. Because there are so many different leaf and flower shapes, unlimited combinations are possible.

All species in this book, except pincushions, dry well, retaining much of their original color and lasting for years. The 1980s saw the beginnings of a booming business in dried proteas emerging from the creative hands of Mauians. A wide variety of flowerhead colors: creams, fawns, greens, pinks, tans, and browns are complemented by "floral furs" in white, rusty, and black. Each basket, wreath, or other arrangement is unique in shape, size, hue, texture, and species composition.

Only the finest flowerheads are chosen for drying. At some farms the flowers and foliage are hung upside-down in darkened rooms containing minimal heat and air-movement. In this manner they dry quickly, without mold, and retain their colors better than if merely hung in the light. If a wreath is desired, flowerheads are gently wired onto foam molds and embellished with baby's breath and foliage (dryandra foliage is popular). No sticky dust-collecting sprays are used.

Home-drying. If you grow proteas or have been given some, dry your own. When the flower-heads lose their freshness, pour off the water and let them dry in the vase. Better still, hang them in a dark location affording a little air-flow. This is especially important if you live in a damp or humid area. They dry more symmetrically if hung upside-down.

Glycerine Preservation. Pound the stems of fresh flowers and place them in a solution composed of one part glycerine, available from any drugstore, to three parts water. In a few days this solution will penetrate the plant's vascular system and appear as beady droplets at the leaf-edges. Remove and place in an upright container. Excess water will evaporate and a shiny, flexible "permanent protea" will remain.

GROWING PROTEAS

Proteas are not tropical plants. Even though they thrive in the Hawaiian Islands, where world standards for flower excellence creep higher with each passing year, proteas only grow at the higher elevations of Maui and the Island of Hawaii (2,000'–4,000'). In the dry or muggy lowlands, they wither and die from fungal diseases and nematode infections.

Proteas are quite fussy about environmental conditions. Unlike hibiscus or daisies, they require very specific geographic and climatic conditions for optimal growth: long, dry summers and short, wet winters (Mediterranean-type climate); night temperatures from 40°F in winter and to around 60°F in summer; warm, dry days most of the year. They also need excellent drainage and acidic, well-aerated soils, not necessarily rich. They particularly favor the gentle, fluctuating airflow and cloud cover regime that is typical of Hawaii's volcanoes.

The hairiest proteas can withstand frosts, bitter winds, and even snow, as they originated in the cold mountains near the southern tip of Africa. On the other hand, banksias, denizens of Australian deserts, exhibit remarkable tolerance to searing heat and desiccation.

However, given specific indoor conditions, proteas will survive and bloom in a variety of climates, as is attested by their early popularity in the royal greenhouses of Europe. Pincushions also grow quite well in California's central valley. If you have questions concerning the purchase of plants, consult any of the farms listed earlier (page 5) or contact the University of Hawaii Agricultural Experiment Research Center, Kula, Maui (808) 878-1213. Proteas are easy — and difficult — to grow. They can weather poor or rocky soils, winds, snow, and droughts, yet may be strangely finicky, suddenly withering and dying for no apparent reason.

A typical day's work at Davis Farm Enterprises, one of the dozens of protea farms on Maui.

Hand-picking pincushions on an early morning in upcountry Maui. Plants are always arranged in neat rows, allowing room for growth.

A typical protea farm in Maui between 2,000 and 4,000' elevation. In the distance lies the Kihei coast, with its six miles of lovely white-sand beaches, and Maalaea Bay to the far right.

Sorting proteas for export.

Picking queen proteas.

A bounty of "pink minks," queen proteas, and banksias.

A radiant mixture of species and colors, including the famous waratah, the state flower of New South Wales, Australia.

ABOUT THE AUTHOR

Dr. Angela Kay Kepler, a naturalized New Zealander, was born in Australia in 1943. It is appropriate that she write a book on proteas and banksias as she has lived and traveled in their native lands, Australia and South Africa. Her home on Maui sits close to the world's leading center for protea farms.

She also grows a variety of proteaceous plants in her large garden.

A writer, photographer, field biologist, biological illustrator, and environmental consultant, she holds degrees from the University of Canterbury, New Zealand; University of Hawaii, Honolulu; and Cornell University, New York.

She has authored several books, and numerous scientific publications, written newspaper columns on biological aspects of the Hawaiian Islands. She has also assisted in forest surveys, seabird studies, and endangered species research in the mainland U.S., Hawaii, West Indies and New Zealand.

ABOUT THE PHOTOGRAPHER

Born and raised on Maui, Jacob R. Mau has recently become nationally and internationally recognized as an outstanding photographer. His photographs, rich with life, color, and design, focus on exotic flowers in Hawaii such as heliconias, gingers, plumerias, proteas and banksias. Notecards and posters of Jacob's work produced by TROPICALS of Alii Gardens, Hana, Maui, are prized by art lovers and horticulturalists alike.

FRONT COVER: Stunning, fuzzy-rimmed "prince proteas" (Protea compacta).
BACK COVER: A three-foot-high "fresh protea in the round,"
by Brooke Bearg and Joan Mercer.

OTHER TITLES BY THE AUTHOR

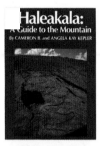

Haleakala: A Guide to the Mountain
by Cameron B. and Angela K. Kepler

The entire mountain, from sun-spangled shorelines through lush lowland forests, verdant pastures and alpine expanses. History, geography cultural events and accommodations, a complete hiking and camping guide, points of interest, day trips and extended hikes. Over 200 color photographs , maps.
ISBN 0-935180-67-2 • 96 pages • 5 3/4" x 8 1/2" • $8.95

Proteas in Hawaii
by Angela K. Kepler
Photography by Jacob Mau

Floral photography at its best with over 200 photographs on this amazing flowering plant family. An authoritative text provides a wealth of information on correct English and scientific names including pronunciation, buying and caring for the plants, flower arrangements, general and historic information.
ISBN 0-935180-66-4 • 80 pages • 5 3/4" x 8 1/2" • $8.95

Maui's Hana Highway: A Visitors Guide
by Angela K. Kepler

The incredible 52-mile journey of 617 curves and 56 bridges through some of Hawaii's most breathtaking scenery. Packed with hundreds of facts and interesting information.
ISBN 0-935180-62-1 • 80 pages • 5 3/4" x 8 1/2" • $8.95

Exotic Tropicals of Hawaii: Heliconias, Gingers, Anthuriums and Decorative Foliage
by Angela Kay Kepler
Photography by Jacob Mau

For the first time ever, a complete account of over 136 species of gingers, heliconias and Hawaii's other "tropicals," including anthuriums, birds-of-paradise, ornamental bananas, fanciful and "jungle foliage." Accompanied by and authoritative text that includes correct English and scientific names, usage, flower arrangement.
ISBN 0-935180-83-4 • 5 3/4" x 8 1/2" • 112 pages • softcover • $9.95

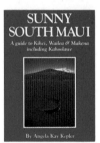

Sunny South Maui by Angela K. Kepler
Hawaii's best-selling author explores Maui's south coastal plains, revealing it to be an area rich in history and nature as well as man-made environs. From Kahului to La Perousse, including Molokini Islet and Kahoolawe. ISBN 1-56647-012-9 • 6" x 9" • 144 pages • Softcover • $13.95

Majestic Molokai: A nature Lover's Guide
by Angela K. Kepler & Cameron B. Kepler

A strong pictorial description of Molokai and its many natural wonders. A conservation message permeates the text, which also includes an appreciation of the ways of the original settlers—the early Hawaiians.
ISBN 0-935180-73-7 • 6" x 9" • 144 pages • softcover • $13.95

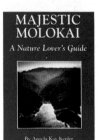

HOW TO ORDER
Send check or money order with a additional $3.00 for the first book and .50 cents for each additional book to cover mailing and handling to:

Mutual Publishing
1127 11th Avenue, Mezz. B
Honolulu, Hawaii 96816
Ph (808) 732-1709 • Fax (808) 734-4094
Email: mutual@lava.net • Url: http://www.pete.com/mutual